To:

_____

From:

_____

Date:

_____

MOSES'
MEMORY BOOK

How God Led His People and Me out of
Egypt and into the Promised Land

Allia Zobel Nolan
Illustrated by Linda Clearwater

HARVEST HOUSE PUBLISHERS

EUGENE, OREGON

Moses' Memory Book

Text Copyright © 2010 by Allia Zobel Nolan
Artwork Copyright © 2010 by Linda Clearwater

Published by Harvest House Publishers
Eugene, Oregon 97402
www.harvesthousepublishers.com

ISBN 978-0-7369-2543-3

Original artwork by Linda Clearwater

Design and production by Mary pat Design, Westport, Connecticut

Visit Allia Zobel Nolan at www.AlliaWrites.com

Scripture quotations are taken from the Good News Translation –
Second Edition © 1992 by American Bible Society. Used by permission.

Printed in China
10 11 12 13 14 15 16 / LP / 10 9 8 7 6 5 4 3 2 1

For God, whose grace helps us all out of sin's bondage and into the Promised Land of His love; my husband, Desmond, whose patience and encouragement are like manna from heaven; and the team at Harvest House, whose help and friendship are worth more than ten Pharaohs' treasures.

Allia Zobel Nolan

Reading this book, I am reminded that the inspiration of a great leader is never self-motivated. There is a force above us all, making even the most powerful of leaders the humblest of followers. I am thankful for those who have led me through my life and also to those who have had the confidence in me to let me lead. The opportunity to do both is truly a blessing.

Linda Clearwater

Dear Friends,

Whenever I think of the story of Moses, dozens of pictures run through my mind. A simple shepherd, he had no wish to be a great leader. He had no desire to travel, and he never dreamed he'd be in the Bible Hall of Fame. In fact, he didn't like public speaking at all and would probably have preferred to sit on a scorpion rather than go and tell the powerful Pharaoh to let God's people go.

But—and here's the great part—once Moses accepted God's plan and his own starring role in it, something wonderful happened. He changed. God's grace surrounded him. Nothing was impossible. With great trust, bravery, patience, courage—and I have to believe a super-sized sense of humor—Moses was able to pull off the "great escape" and lead thousands of God's complaining people on a 40-day trip that lasted 40 years.

You and I can learn a lot from Moses. But one lesson stands out from the rest—God may ask you to do something that might seem impossible or something you just don't want to do. When that happens, think of Moses and remember God knows more about His plan for your life than you do. And if you accept and trust Him, chances are you'll find God can make the impossible possible for you too.

Allia Zobel Nolan

CHAPTER 1

I guess it all started on a mountain. That's where God spoke to me. I'm standing there when I see flames coming from a bush, but the leaves aren't burning up.

I take a step closer, and that's when I hear this voice call, "MO-SES!"

It was God all right. But just in case I had any doubts, the voice says, "I am the God of your father, the God of Abraham, the God of Isaac, and the God of Jacob."

"Yes, Lord, I get it," I answer. "But what is it You would have me do?"

"Well, Moses, " God answers, "I need you to speak to Pharaoh. Tell him, 'God says, Let my people go!'"

I hear this, and I almost faint.

"Are you thinking of the same Pharaoh I'm thinking of, Lord?" I ask. "The Pharaoh who wears a hissing cobra on his head and has hundreds of soldiers with swords, chariots, and big muscles protecting him? That Pharaoh?"

The mighty king of Egypt with some of his men.

"Yes, Moses," God says, "that very one."

"But, Lord," I protest, "I'm just a simple shepherd. You need a really high-powered guy for *that* job."

"No, Moses," God says, "I need you." Then God tells me to go to His people and explain that He's going to save them.

"And if they want to know Your name, Lord?" I ask God.

Tell them 'I AM' sent you," God says.

"But what if they don't believe me, Lord?" I say.

God says, "Then this is what I want you to do."

God tells me His name is "I AM."

CHAPTER 2

God tells me to throw my staff on the ground. I do, and the staff becomes a snake. Then God tells me to pick up the snake by its tail. I do and the snake becomes my staff again.

"When they see that," God says, "they'll believe."

My staff becomes a snake. Ewwwww!

Okay, I think to myself, *I might convince the Israelites with my snake staff, but ME telling the king of Egypt to let his slaves go? He'll have me fried in oil or, worse, tickled to death. Oy veh.*

"Ah, God," I answer finally, "You know I'm a shy guy. Please, I beg You! Pick someone else!"

"Look, Moses," God answers, "I love you, but you're not being very cooperative at the moment. You have a brother. Well, he'll go along with you. AND THAT'S THE END OF IT, YES?"

"Yes, Lord," I say, knowing there's no way I'm going to win.

So Aaron and I head off to the Israelite elders and tell them God is setting His people free. The good news is they believe us. Then we go to Pharaoh's palace. He isn't so agreeable.

"The Lord wants *me* to let *my* slaves go?" says Pharaoh, eyebrows raised and a smirk on his face. "What Lord?" he asks. *"I'm* the only lord around here. Got that? And I'm *not* going to let the slaves go, but I *will* make it harder for them to stay.

Me telling the elders the good news.

"From now on, they will not only make bricks to build my buildings," Pharaoh says, "but they will also collect the hay to make the bricks as well. And no drop in productivity, you hear? As for you two, you'd better scram, or I'll put you to work with the rest of them!"

CHAPTER 3

"Now look what you've done!" the elders scream at us. "You've made things worse!"

The elders yelling at Aaron and me.

So I excuse myself and call on the Lord.

"See, Lord?" I say. "I told You I'd just foul things up. Instead of letting the people go, Pharaoh is working them harder."

"Trust me, Moses," God says. "Go back to Pharaoh and insist."

When Aaron and I return to the palace, Pharaoh is sitting there, surrounded by advisors and magicians.

Aaron and I smack in the middle of a bunch of snakes.

"The Lord wants you to let His people go," I say. "And here is His sign."

At that, Aaron throws down the staff, and it turns into a snake. But a minute later, Pharaoh's magicians do the same thing. So here we are in the middle of a bunch of ugly, wriggly snakes, and I'm feeling sick when—GULP!—Aaron's snake swallows up the magicians' snakes.

"Is that the best you can do?" says Pharaoh.

"Let God's people go, or you shall see," Aaron answers.

"Not a chance," says Pharaoh. His heart is as hard as ten stone sphinxes.

With that the duel is on. I don't know how many plagues God has up His sleeve, but I'm not looking forward to finding out. I wish there were some way I could convince Pharaoh to listen. I'm thinking, *Maybe Aaron isn't taking the right approach. Maybe I'll try this time.*

CHAPTER 4

So I say, "You know, Pharaoh, it's not me who wants the slaves to go free. It's God Almighty. So how about it? Let God's people go, huh?"

"Is there something about 'no' that you don't understand, Moses?" says Pharaoh.

So Aaron stretches out his staff, and the Nile turns red.

"Still not impressed," says Pharaoh, as his magicians raise their staffs, and the Nile becomes even bloodier.

Pharaoh's magician uses his staff to turn the Nile water to blood, just as Aaron did.

Me begging Pharaoh to let God's people go.

"Oy veh," I say to Aaron. "Maybe we should come back tomorrow."

"Let God's people go, pretty please?" I plead with Pharaoh at our next meeting, after which the king's parrot takes up the call. "Let God's people go," he squawks.

"Never," says Pharaoh, and I'm beginning to believe him.

So, Aaron raises his staff, and God sends frogs.

"All right!" says Pharaoh. "Get rid of the frogs, and the slaves can go." But as soon as God does this, Pharaoh takes back his word.

"Na-na-na-na-na-na," he teases me. "Your precious Israelites are staying right where they are."

So God sends teeny-tiny gnats, big-eyed flies, and a horrible sickness that attacks the animals. Then He causes everyone to break out with boils and sends storms and hail.

Each time Pharaoh says, "Okay, go," a half hour later, things return to normal, and he says, "No, you can't go."

CHAPTER 5

So God sends a wind filled with locusts, and a zillion hungry insects eat up everything. After that there's a three-day blackout, and the days are so dark, you can't see your hand in front of your face.

God makes sure this bad stuff only happens to the Egyptians.

"Thanks, God," I say because there are two things I really can't stand—one is a frog in my bed and the other is a fly in my soup.

"No problem," God says, "but I need you to give My people some instructions. Tell them to sprinkle the blood of a lamb over their doors. They are to eat its meat roasted with bitter herbs along with unleavened bread. And they must eat quickly."

God's people painting their doors with blood.

"Got it, Lord," I stammer.

That night there's an eerie silence as God sends the last plague. While I lie there with one eye open, the angel passes over us but strikes down every firstborn of Egypt—even the animals. And when Pharaoh hears his son is dead, his hardened heart breaks. He gives up and calls for me.

"It's over," he says. "Get out. Take the slaves. Go!"

So I do.

"Any particular reason, Lord?" I ask.

"I'm sending the angel of death to Egypt tonight," God says.

"Don't worry, Moses. He will pass over the doors that are marked. And, Moses," the Lord continues, "tell the people they are to make this Passover meal every year as a reminder of the night I set them free."

After Pharaoh's son dies, he tells me to go!

CHAPTER 6

Meanwhile, as word spreads, the men grab their wives. The wives grab their children. The children grab their grannies and grandpas, their cats and favorite toys, and with every family's sheep trailing behind them, we quickly skedaddle out of Egypt.

Aaron figuring out how long our journey will be.

"Well, that went smoothly," says Aaron. "Now all you have to do is lead the people to the Promised Land. My guesstimate is there are about 600,000 men plus their wives and children." Then he whips out his abacus and makes the beads fly. "Barring any traffic, attacks, or sandstorms, we should make it there in about 40 days."

"Which way, Lord?" I ask because I'm really bad with directions.

"Take the back roads, Moses," God says. "Head toward the Red Sea. We'll avoid any local wars that way. Don't worry because I'll be ahead of you in a cloud during the day and at your back in a pillar of fire at night."

"Okay, Lord," I say, "copy that."

Everyone is in a good mood, and we make great time leaving Egypt. I see people dancing and hear them singing. Even the animals are smiling. Soon we hear the ocean waves breaking.

Suddenly I feel the ground shake. Then I hear what sounds like a hundred elephants with armor.

"Lord," I call out, "tell me it isn't true! Not him again?"

I look back, and sure enough, a wild-eyed Pharaoh and his army are coming straight for us. I hear the *click-click* of the Israelites' teeth chattering.

"We're trapped!" a woman shouts. "SAVE US!"

"Don't worry!" I scream at the top of my lungs. "God will protect us!"

CHAPTER 7

"Ah, God," I say, my voice quaking, "any ideas?"

"Raise your staff over the water," God says. So I do.

Then I hear a strong wind blowing and loud voices behind me shouting, "Praise be God who delivers us!"

I squint into the distance and can't believe my eyes. The sea is divided right down the middle, like a part in the center of a child's hair. I can see the ocean floor. I look at the people, and they're not moving. So I put my fingers in my mouth and let out a whistle you can hear in Galilee.

"Yo, people!" I yell, "What are you waiting for?" With that the crowd runs across the bottom of the seabed, and I'm right behind them.

But Pharaoh's army follows and starts gaining on us.

"Stretch out your hand again, Moses," God says. So I do, and the water tumbles down in a great big SPLASH! Unfortunately, that's the end of Pharaoh's army. After such a close call, I am glad to join the others, praising God for saving us yet again.

The sea closes up on Pharaoh and his men.

The Israelites have short memories, though. We aren't out of Egypt three months when the kvetchers start kvetching.

"It's hot. I'm thirsty. And there is *way* too much sand in this desert," they whine. "We never should have left. At least in Egypt we had food. We had water. We had Saturday night chariot races."

The Israelites complaining to me again.

"So you'd prefer being slaves," I ask, "carrying heavy bricks in the blazing sun?"

"It wasn't *that* bad," a teenager answers. "I lost a lot of weight. I got a good tan."

I take a deep breath and sigh. Now I see what God puts up with.

CHAPTER 8

"We're going to die!" one woman shouts. "And it's all your fault, Moses."

"Oy veh, and what isn't?" I answer. Then I gather the crowd around. "Listen," I say, "God really loves you people. He has told me this a million times. So you think He'd let you starve? Or die of thirst? Have a little faith," I say.

"I know you're hungry," I continue, "and I'll definitely check with God about the food situation. But in the meantime, let's stay focused on the Lord's goodness. Okay, people?"

"Okay, Moses," they say, and the crowd stops grumbling and starts going back to their chores.

"Don't worry about the food and water," God says. "I'll take care of everything."

"Thanks. I knew you would, God," I say.

That night the wind blows hundreds of birds called *quail* into the camp. The next morning, snow-like flakes cover the ground. The Israelites see it and say, "What is it?"

A little girl puts some into her mouth, and says, "I don't know what it is, Mommy, but it tastes yummy, like wafers made with honey. I'm going to eat it."

"See? God hasn't forgotten you," I explain to the Israelites. "You have your food. It may not be corned beef on rye, but there was meat last night, and today He's sent you a special kind of bread. So don't worry. God takes care of you. He knows what you need. And He will always provide for you."

God drops bread-like food from the sky.

Folks are feeling better now. Their bellies are full of quail and *manna* (this is what we call the honey wafers). And after God shows me how to get water from a rock, we're back on the road again. God is so amazing.

God's people eat the quail and manna God sends.

21

CHAPTER 9

We arrive at Mount Sinai, and God wants me to give the Israelites a message. "Tell them if they obey Me," He says, "I'll be their God, and they'll be My treasure."

I tell the Israelites, and the people all say, "We will keep the Lord's commands. We want to be His people."

Later God has another request. "Moses, I want you to lead the people to the foot of the mountain. And I will talk to you from a thick cloud."

So the people wash their clothes, shine their sandals, and put on their best jewelry. For three days they wait patiently. Then a trumpet blasts across the land. The mountain shakes, and thunder goes BA-BOOM, BA-BOOM, BA-BOOM!

Me climbing up the mountain to talk with God.

"This is it!" I shout to them. "Follow me!" I can see fear in their faces, but we hurry to the base of the mountain. There, God appears in a huge cloud and tells me to come up to Him. With my superior hamstrings I'm up the mountain in no time. That's when God gives the Israelites His rules. "I am the Lord your God," God says. "These are My commands:"

You shall have no other gods before Me.

You shall worship Me and not make idols.

You shall not misuse My name.

You shall keep the Sabbath holy.

You shall honor your father and mother.

You shall not murder.

You shall be faithful to your husband or wife.

You shall not steal.

You shall not tell lies about others.

You shall not long for what belongs to others.

God writes these rules on two stone tablets and hands them to me. Then He tells me that He has more laws to give to the Israelites. So time flies, and before I realize it, I am away for 40 days. I am so overjoyed at being with God, I don't give the time another thought until I get an uneasy feeling, like someone is talking about me...

CHAPTER 10

"Moses-Schmoses," says one of the elders. "Where has he gone anyway? We don't need him. Let's make some gods of our own. They can lead us out of this mess."

Aaron collects jewelry to make a false god.

"Aaron," the man calls out, "looks like your brother isn't coming back. So we need you to make us a god—something in gold and with horns would be nice."

Meanwhile, God sees what's going on and says to me, "You'd better leave now, Moses, because *your* people are bowing down to a statue of a cow. Your brother helped them make it."

"Oy veh," I say, "God, I'm so sorry."

"I'm sorry too, Moses," God continues, "because you know I'm a patient God. But My anger is burning against your people, and I think it's time to destroy them." *This is it.* I think to myself. *God is finished with the Israelites. I have to act fast.*

"God," I say, "please forgive them."

"Lord" I continue, "if not for these people, do it for Your servants Abraham, Isaac, and Jacob. Remember, You *promised* to make them a great nation."

And with that, the Lord holds back His anger.

"Lord," I say, "You are a merciful, loving God, and I thank You." Then I grab the tablets and go. Halfway down the mountain, I see Israelites dancing around a golden idol. Before you can say "Wait until I get my hands on Aaron," I fling the tablets and— CA-RASH—they shatter on the rocks. Then I run to camp and burn the idol until it's a smoldering pile of dust.

"They made me do it," Aaron lies when I take him aside.

"Well, I hope you can control yourself and them," I yell, "because now I have to go back up and get another set of God's rules!"

CHAPTER *11*

So up I go again, and now my hamstrings are starting to smart.

"The people say they'll behave," I tell God. "They say they're sorry. So please, Lord, go ahead of us."

In His mercy, God says, "Yes." He'll go with us. Then He gives me instructions for building a holy place—a tabernacle—for Him. When I climb down, I tell the Israelites that God has forgiven them again.

"We will do whatever the Lord commands," the Israelites assure me, but I have my doubts. Then off we go, with God's glory filling the tabernacle. Things are going well until...

"NO MORE MANNA!" yell some troublemakers, stirring up the Israelite camp. "MEAT! MEAT! MEAT! GIVE US MEAT!"

I turn and go to my tent.

Some Israelites complain because they want different food to eat.

"Lord," I say boldly, "it's never enough with these people. They say they're sick of the food You sent. Help me, please!"

So God makes a strong wind blow, and once again quail appear as far as the eye can see.

"Now we're talking!" a grinning troublemaker shouts. Then a gang of the complainers run and grab the birds out of the sky. They cook the fowl, stuff themselves silly, get terrible tummy aches, and die. After that, the Israelites eat God's manna and keep quiet.

God sends thousands of quail. Complainers pick them from the sky.

Okay, so finally we near the land of Canaan, and God tells me to send some men to explore it. I order scouts, including two of my best soldiers, Caleb and Joshua, to go out and see what they can see. After 40 days, they return. The news isn't good.

"The soldiers are nine feet tall," one scout says, "and they're built like Pharaoh's gladiators. Plus the city's surrounded by huge walls. It's suicide. We'll get slaughtered."

CHAPTER 12

I listen, but I can't help thinking, *A bunch of old ladies, these Israelites are. Don't they realize a few soldiers with muscles are no match for the Lord? When are they going to learn that nothing is impossible with God?*

Soon word spreads that the new land is filled with pumped-up Goliaths, who chew through armor like butter and eat their enemies' heads for breakfast. And that's just the women. So the people reject the land God wants to give them.

"We'd rather die in the desert than fight these monsters," an Israelite elder crows. "Let's just pick another leader and head back to Egypt."

But then Joshua and Caleb speak up.

Joshua and Caleb talking about the Promised Land.

"Moses," Caleb says, addressing the crowd as well as me, "this land is good because the Lord God has picked it for us."

"So it stands to reason," Joshua continues, "if God is giving us this land, He will go before us and help us defeat these people."

"Bravo, you guys!" I say. "At last, somebody gets it!"

But it's too late. God hears that the Israelites refuse to enter Canaan, and His anger burns. So the deal is off. With the exception of Caleb and Joshua, no Promised Land for the Israelites. Instead, God tells me that it will go to the children. Needless to say, everyone is really upset. But they brought it on themselves.

"Ah, so where does that leave us, God?" I ask.

"Back to the desert, Moses," God says, "but don't worry. I'll be with you."

"Oy veh," I say. "Here we go again."

Me hitting my head in frustration.

CHAPTER 13

I'm now 120 years old. We're back at the Jordan River, and we're set to cross over to Canaan. God takes me up the mountain and shows me the lush, green Promised Land. I look at it and smile.

"Lord, it's more beautiful than any land I've ever seen, and I'm happy we finally made it. So what now, Lord?" I ask.

God suggests I take an early retirement and hand over my staff to Joshua, who will lead the Israelites into Canaan.

"Good choice, Lord," I say with relief. "He'll make a great leader. He's got superb hamstrings."

"Oh, and God," I say, "there's one more thing. You know I really didn't want this job, but I'm so very glad You insisted because I had the time of my life. And I learned a lot: to trust You, carry a big stick, eat the white stuff, quit worrying, be grateful, never complain, have patience, skip the quail, and retire early.

"But it was seeing how strong Your love is for Your people that has left the greatest impression on me. I witnessed, up-front, what a wondrous, forgiving, patient God You are, and I'll never forget that."

Me thanking God for my wonderful adventure.

When I return to camp, there's a big-city publishing agent sitting inside my tent.

"Moses," she says, "we'd love to do a book about your adventures. Do you think you can remember it all?"

"Oy veh," I say. "This is one story I'll NEVER forget. But there's something I really need to do first," I tell her.

What's that?" she asks.

"Soak my feet."

THE END

GLOSSARY

A
abacus—an instrument people use to add and subtract numbers by moving sliders back and forth on rods

E
eerie—kind of scary or frightening

G
Goliath—the more-than-nine-foot-tall Philistine warrior whom young David conquered (see 1 Samuel 17); also if a person calls someone a "Goliath," that person thinks the other is really tall and strong

H
hamstrings—muscles or tendons that are located in the back of the leg

I
idol—a false god; can be any object, figure, statue, or image people make and then pray to and worship

M
manna—the white bread-like food God sent down from heaven to the Israelites so they would have food to eat while in the desert; the word literally means "What is it?"

O
oy veh—a Bible-time Hebrew saying used much like "Oh boy!" or "Oh brother!" or "Oh gosh!" and meaning you don't believe something, you are in shock, or you are annoyed

P
Pharaoh—the name of the kings of Egypt back in Bible times
productivity—the amount of something you make

Q
quail—small, brown-spotted birds that are part of the pheasant family; along with the manna, God sent quail to the Israelites to eat while they were in the desert

S
Sabbath—seventh day of the week; a day to rest and worship God
sovereign—someone in a high position; another name for the Pharaoh
sphinx—an Egyptian statue that has the body of a lion and the head of a man

T
tongue-tied—a description of someone who can't seem to find or speak the right words, as if his or her tongue was tied

"The Israelites had lived in Egypt for 430 years. On the day the 430 years ended, all the tribes of the LORD's people left Egypt."

Exodus 12:40-41